especially for

Ann

Courage
Doesn't
always
Roar

Courage Doesn't Always Roar

mary anne radmacher

Conari Press

First published in 2009 by Conari Press,
an imprint of Red Wheel/Weiser, LLC
With offices at:
500 Third Street, Suite 230
San Francisco, CA 94107
www.redwheelweiser.com

ISBN: 978-1-57324-410-7
Library of Congress Cataloging-in-Publication Data available upon request.

Cover and text design by Jessica Dacher
Typeset in Agenda
Cover illustrations and hand lettering by Mary Anne Radmacher

Printed in Hong Kong
SS
10 9 8 7 6 5 4 3 2 1

Courage doesn't always roar
Sometimes courage is the quiet voice
at the end of the day saying,
"I will try again tomorrow."

To the adoptive mom who inspired the original phrase; to the firehouses who posted the phrase above their doors after 9/11; to the health and service industry workers, the teachers, the health professionals, the students, who look at this statement before they walk out their door; to the bloggers and speakers and writers who align these words with their own work—I dedicate this to you all who understand the difference between explicitly expecting success and working in a construct where to "try again" requires the deepest courage of all.

Courage resides in the workplace, in the places we play, where we dwell, and all the spots in between. If you are willing, you will see courage in everyday sorts of spaces. In that "everydayness," courage is both ordinary and extraordinary.

Courage has color—brilliant sun and luminous moon. Courage is the purple press of dusk with miles to go before you reach home. It is the color of spring pushing against the lingering winter. It is the indigo sea over which dreams are whispered. It is the weaving of all these colors into a tapestry that reminds us that we are braver than we know and stronger than we ever imagined.

Courage has sound—it comes as a whisper and sometimes a roar. It is the quick expulsion of air, barely audible, blown before changing from an old way to a new. It is the trembled "oh," which comes before you do that thing you think you cannot do, and then it's the sound you make after you do it.

Courage has form—a broad brushstroke and a tiny mark. It is dressed in symbols and specifics. It appears transformative as a butterfly and it is unrepeatable, like a snowflake. It is deeply rooted and reaching ever up, as a tree.

Courage is a paradox. Courage is the willingness to aspire, reach, and again believe in the promise of tomorrow.

Courage . . .

doesn't always roar.

Sometimes

courage is the
quiet voice

at the end
of the day
saying,

"I will try again tomorrow."

It takes courage

to change
your
style,

your
opinion,

the path
you
walk...

your hat!

It takes courage to let go

of the
weighty parts
of your
past.

It takes courage
to find
your own
voice.

to reinvent joys,

to reinvent
opportunities,

to reinvent
dreams,

to reinvent connections ...

to reinvent
hopes
that you have
set
aside.

It takes courage

to recognize
that rigid
habit inhibits.

It takes courage to accept

that the
way you
"have always
been__"

does not determine the way you are.

It takes courage

to
stand
in a
place
you didn't know
existed...

and
learn
from a
view

you
previously
couldn't
imagine.

It takes
courage
to
let
go

of

your

assumptions

and
fly
your
dreams
as a

soaring?
invitation
to become
the best
version of
yourself.

It takes courage to stand for your convictions.

It takes
courage
to
give up
control.

and it takes
courage
to recognize
you are
perfect

just the way you are.

Change,
of
any sort,

requires
courage...

courage
to write
a new story
of your
life

with the

pen

of each

day

...of
every
moment.

Tell yourself
this little story
when you
need it -

"I have
the
courage
to
stand

in whatever
the
weather
brings...

and
understand
that
everything
is
washable____.

everything

is

fixable

and
everything
is
replaceable

but
my
time and
breath. "

The
opportunity
for
greater
courage

comes in
the most
ordinary
of moments.

Courage sings the praises

of the
sturdy souls
and says to
them,

"Today
I will borrow
a little
of your
courage

and see what
garden I can
& water
with the
healing
of my tears;

and what
growing things
I can
nurture
with the
strength of my
laughter."

Courage
is defined more
by its contrasts
than its
samenesses,

more by its
~~risks~~
than its security

Courage
is
content
to make no
excuses.

Courage, dressed in intentional change, is the most ferocious response to fear.

Courage acts without regret

Courage
Laughs
Oright
out loud.

Have the courage to walk out the door and

Let
possibilities
discover
you.

Have the
courage
to wander
and parades
will find
you.

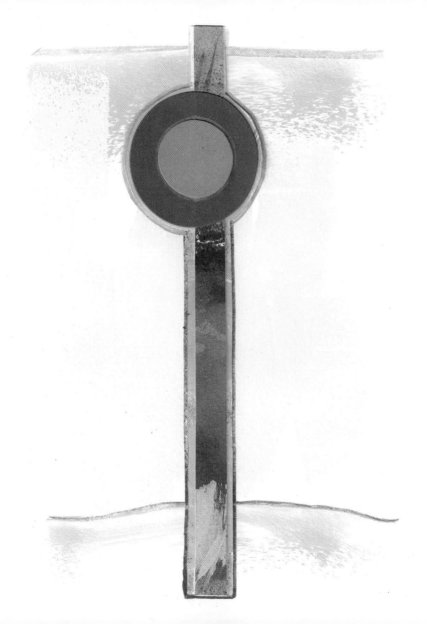

Courage.

as you weigh
the
many
possibilities
of your
day

measure
your
action
with this
question,

"How would I most like to remember this?"

Your
chosen
answer
becomes

your
natural
action
and

Your unique opportunity for courage.

Perspective
in the large.

Grace in the
small.

an open hand.

a practiced pause.

a YES!

Courage
doesn't always
roar.

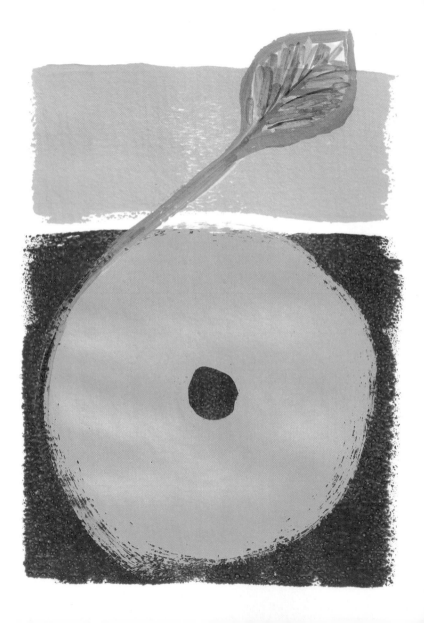